creative
THERAPY
AN ANTI-STRESS
COLOURING
—BOOK—

Michael O'Mara Books Limited

Illustrated by Hannah Davies, Richard Merritt and Jo Taylor

Edited by Lauren Farnsworth

Cover design by John Bigwood

Designed by Zoe Bradley & Jack Clucas

With additional material adapted from www.shutterstock.com

The material in this book was first published in a hardback edition in 2014 by Michael O'Mara Books.

First published in this edition in Great Britain in 2015 by Michael O'Mara Books Limited,
9 Lion Yard, Tremadoc Road, London SW4 7NQ

www.mombooks.com
Michael O'Mara Books
@OMaraBooks

A CIP catalogue record for this book is available from the British Library.

ISBN: 978-1-78243-444-3

2 4 6 8 10 9 7 5 3

This book was printed in July 2015 by L.E.G.O.,
Viale dell'Industria 2, 36100, Vicenza, Italy.

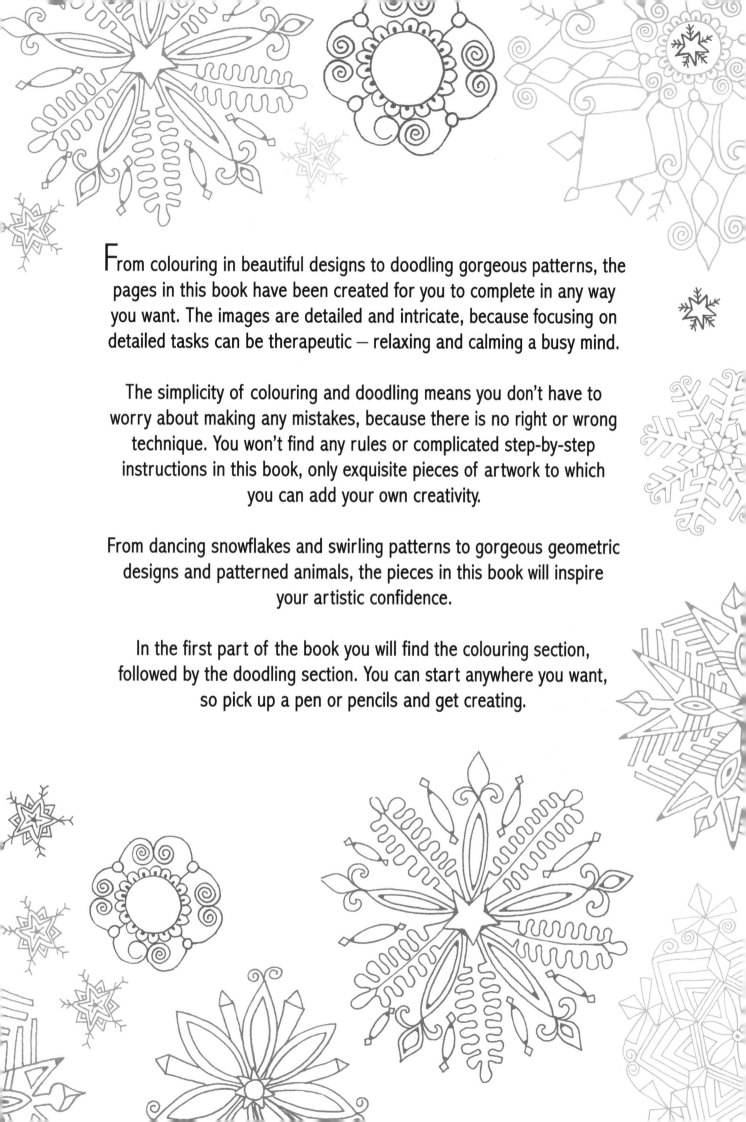

From colouring in beautiful designs to doodling gorgeous patterns, the pages in this book have been created for you to complete in any way you want. The images are detailed and intricate, because focusing on detailed tasks can be therapeutic — relaxing and calming a busy mind.

The simplicity of colouring and doodling means you don't have to worry about making any mistakes, because there is no right or wrong technique. You won't find any rules or complicated step-by-step instructions in this book, only exquisite pieces of artwork to which you can add your own creativity.

From dancing snowflakes and swirling patterns to gorgeous geometric designs and patterned animals, the pieces in this book will inspire your artistic confidence.

In the first part of the book you will find the colouring section, followed by the doodling section. You can start anywhere you want, so pick up a pen or pencils and get creating.

COLOURING

You can use pencils, pens or any colouring method you want in this section. These drawings contain detailed patterns that can be filled in carefully bit by bit, or shaded over to create an area of solid colour.

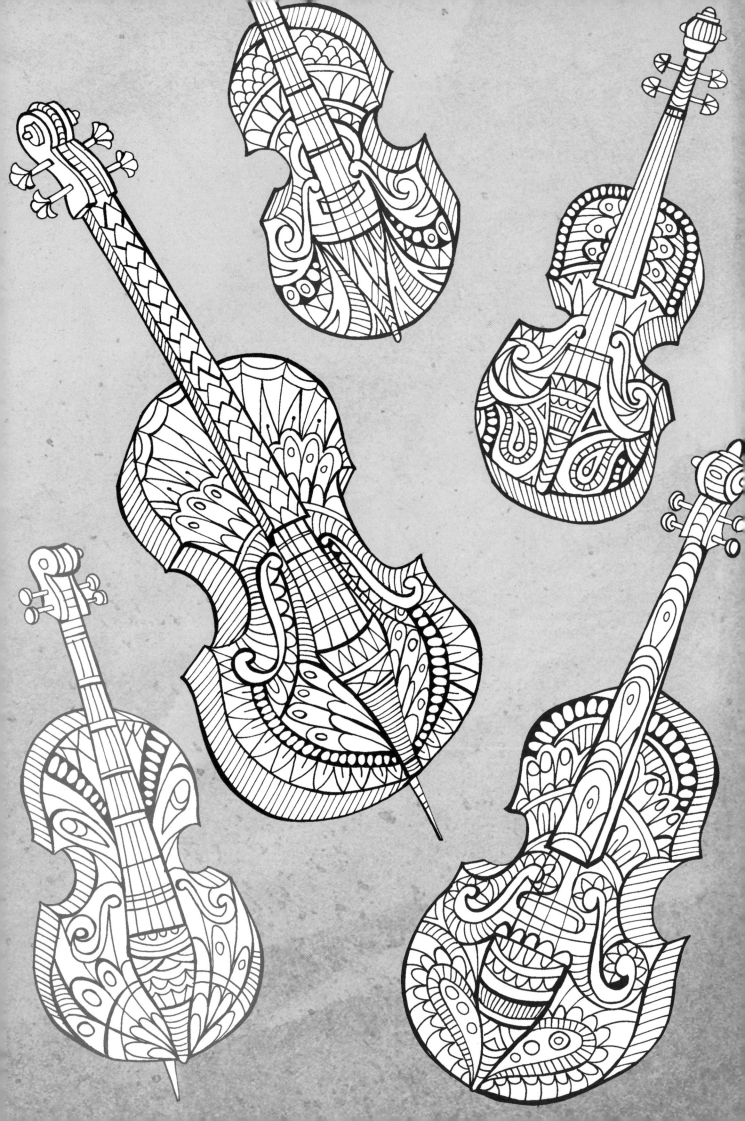

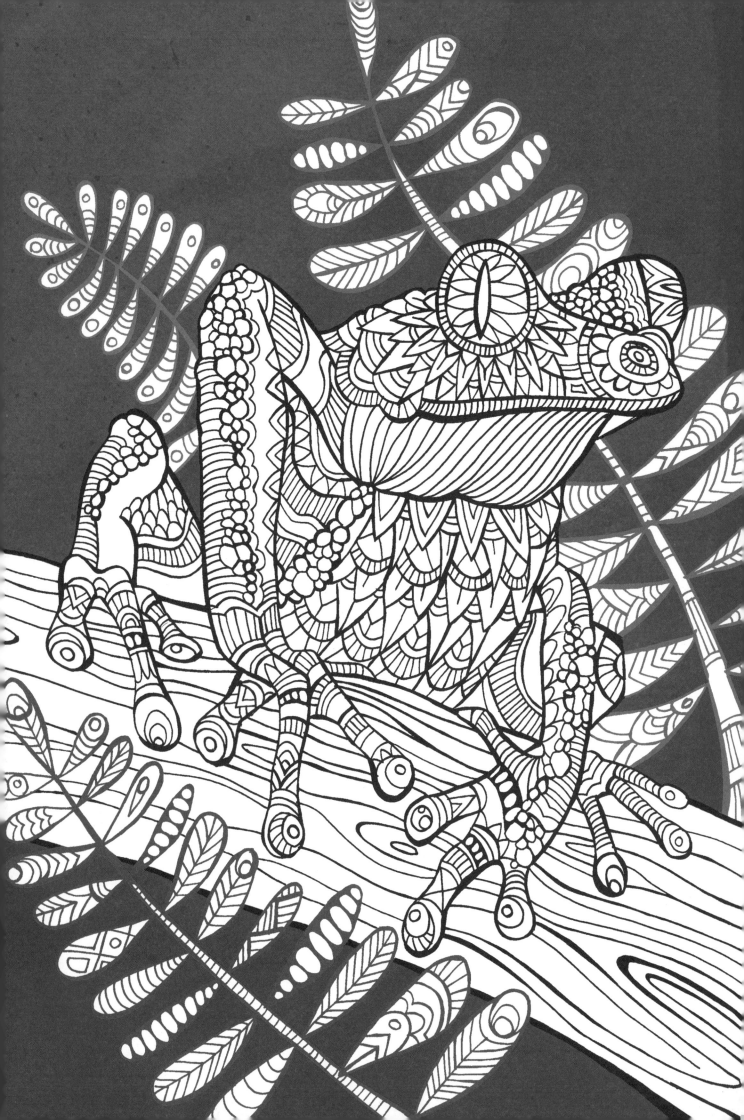

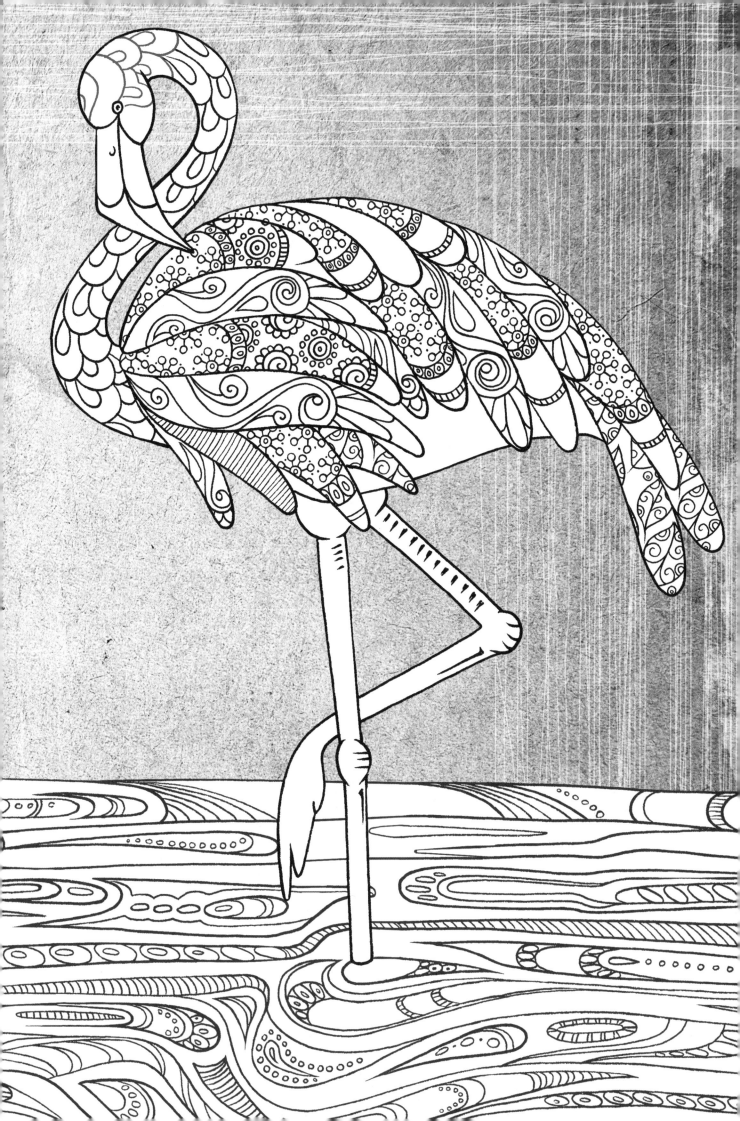

DOODLING

Pick up your colouring pens or pencils and doodle away on the following pages. You can use straight lines, wavy lines, squiggles, patterns – you can't make any mistakes because the choice is yours and the drawings can be completed however you wish.

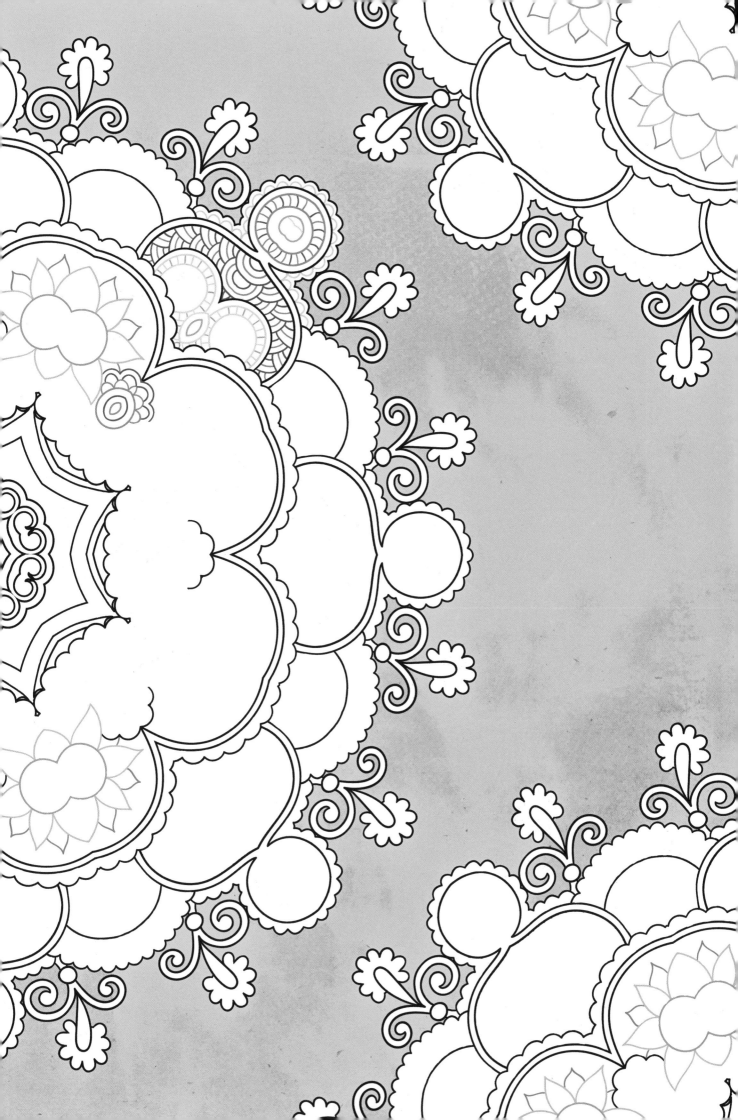

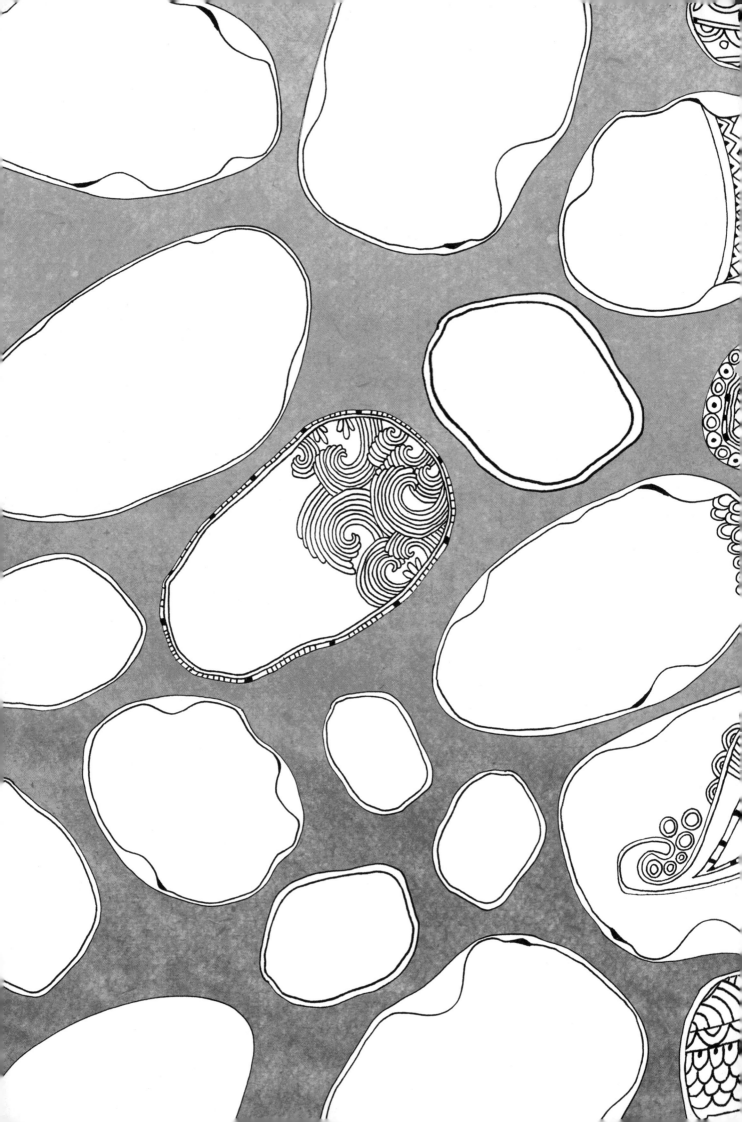

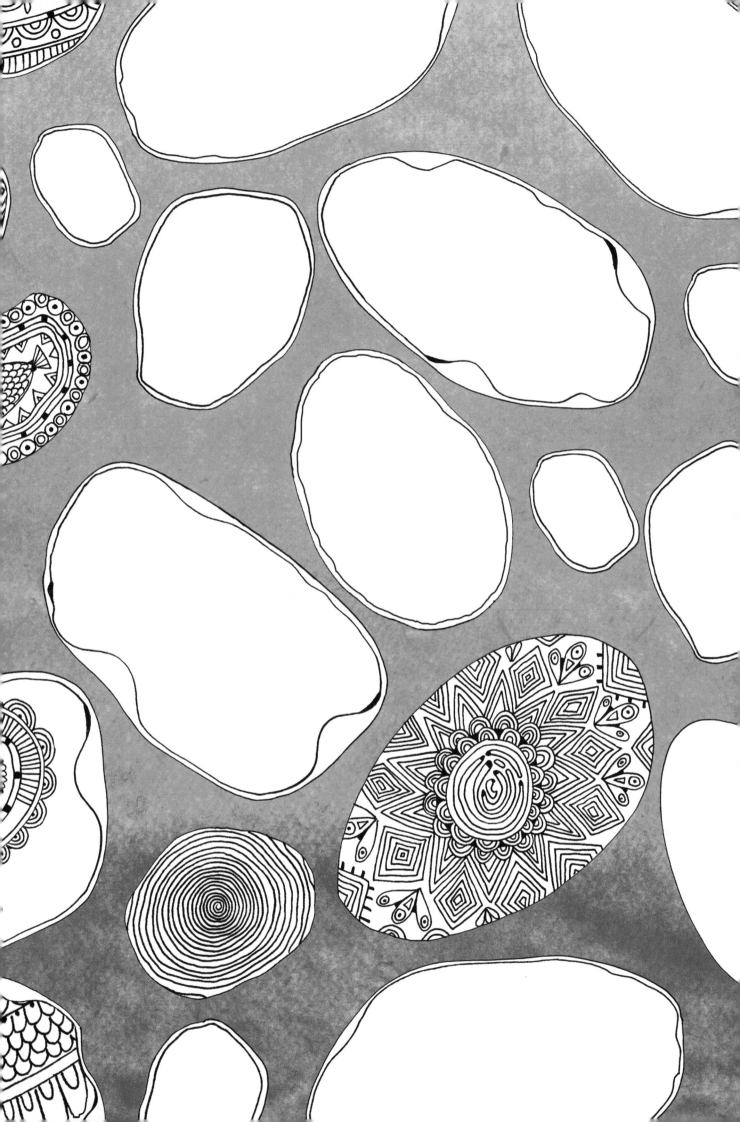